MY PUPPY IS BORN

JOANNA COLE

MY PUPPY IS BORN

PHOTOGRAPHS BY

MARGARET MILLER

REVISED AND EXPANDED EDITION

Morrow Junior Books / New York

To Patti Kirigan and Booboo
J.C.
To Max-Well's Meadowlark Lucy
M.M.

ACKNOWLEDGMENT
Special thanks to Hannah Spector
for her patience, good humor, and love of dogs.
It was always a pleasure to photograph her.

Note: The dogs in this book
are Norfolk terriers.

The photographs were reproduced from
35-mm slides and printed in full color.
The typeface is 16 point Aster.

Printed in Singapore by Tien Wah Press, 1991.
HC   2   3   4   5   6   7   8   9   10
PA 1   2   3   4   5   6   7   8   9   10
Library of Congress Cataloging-in-Publication Data
Cole, Joanna.
My puppy is born/by Joanna Cole ; photographs by Margaret Miller.
—Rev. and expanded ed.
p.   cm.
Summary: Text and photographs follow a Norfolk terrier puppy from
birth to eight weeks later when she goes home with her joyous new owner.
ISBN 0-688-09770-7.—ISBN 0-688-09771-5 (lib. bdg.)—0-688-10198-4 (pbk.)
1. Puppies—Juvenile literature.   2. Norfolk terrier—Juvenile
literature.   [1. Norfolk terrier.   2. Dogs.]   I. Miller, Margaret,
1945–   ill.   II. Title.
SF426.5.C64   1991
636.7'07—dc20   90-42011   CIP   AC

MY PUPPY IS BORN

Guess what?

The dog next door
is having puppies.
And I'm getting one!

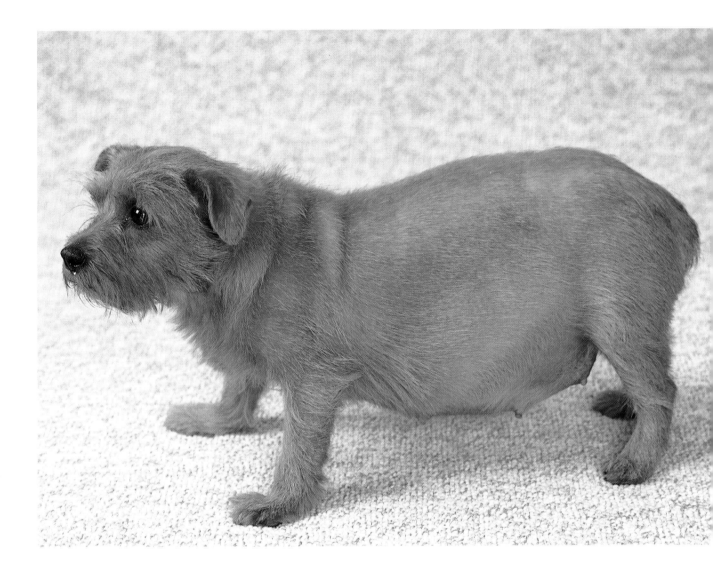

There are lots of puppies
inside her.
Soon they will be born.
I can hardly wait.

When the day arrives,
the mother dog goes to her box.
The torn-up papers make a soft nest.

The mother dog's muscles work hard
to push the first puppy out.

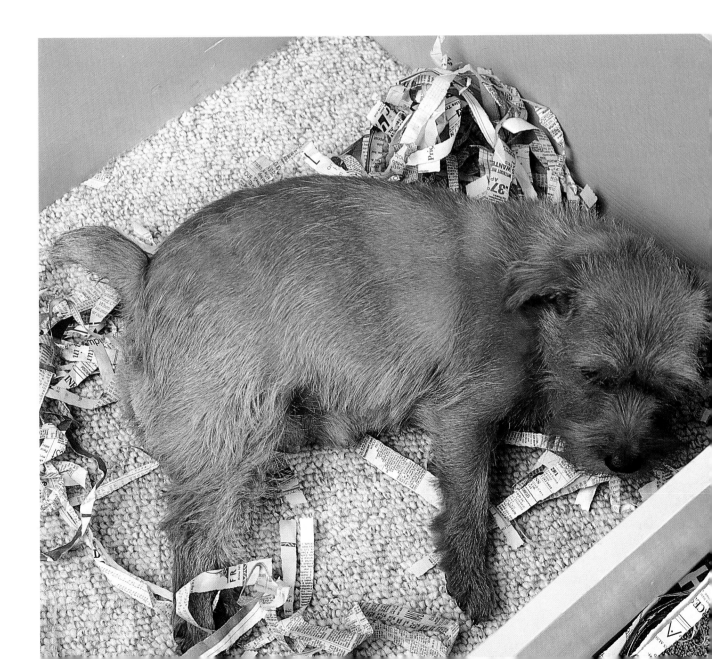

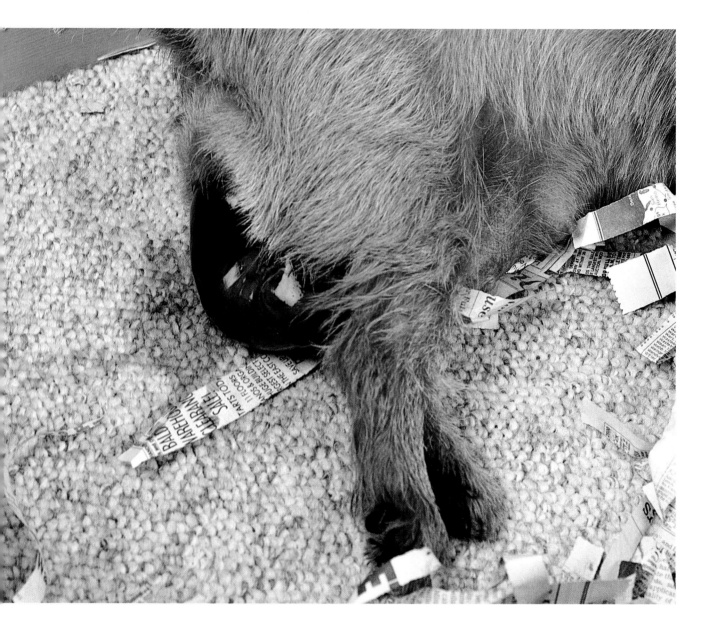

The first puppy is coming.
It is born inside a thin sac.

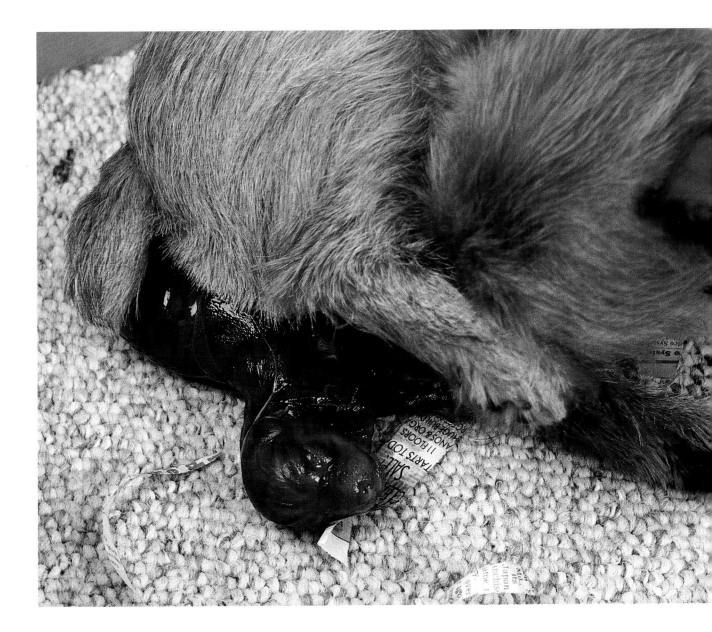

The mother dog has torn open the sac
with her teeth.
Now you can see the newborn puppy.

The puppy is still attached to its mother
by a white tube called the "umbilical cord."
Before the puppy was born,
it got food and oxygen through this cord.

The mother has bitten through the cord.
Now the puppy must eat and breathe
on its own.

The mother dog licks the puppy
until it is all clean.

Then it is time for a rest.
Being born is hard work!

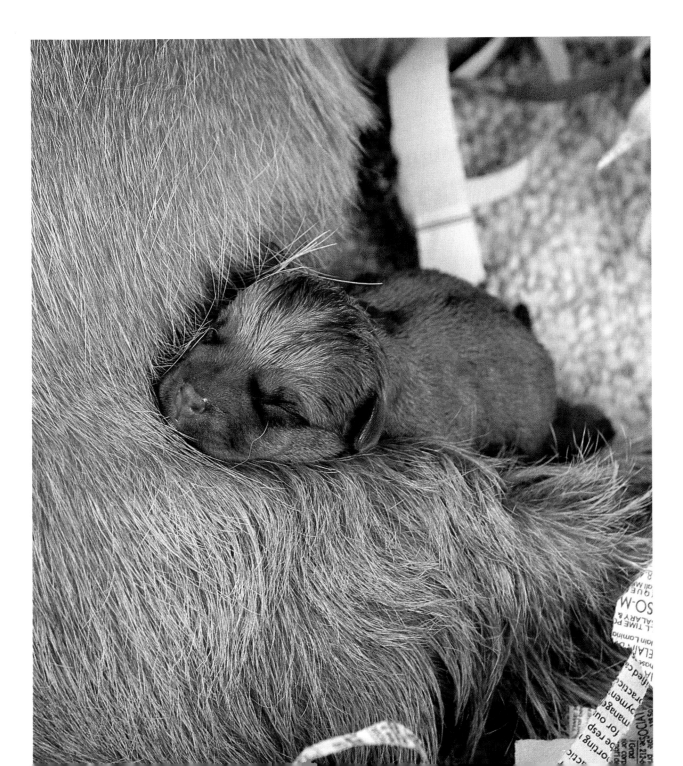

At last all the puppies are born.
The mother dog stays close to them.
She lets them nurse.
She keeps them clean.
She makes sure her babies
have plenty of peace and quiet.

The puppies are *all* wonderful.
But I have decided
this one is going to be mine.
I think I'll name her Dolly.

Dolly is very small.
She weighs only a few ounces.

Dolly can't see. Her eyes won't open yet.
She can't hear, either. Her ears are plugged.

Dolly is too weak to walk. She can only crawl.
She's not ready for solid food. She has no teeth.

But she knows how to nurse already.
If you put your finger in her mouth,
she starts to suck.

When her mother is near,
Dolly crawls around . . .

until she finds a nipple.
Then she starts sucking milk.

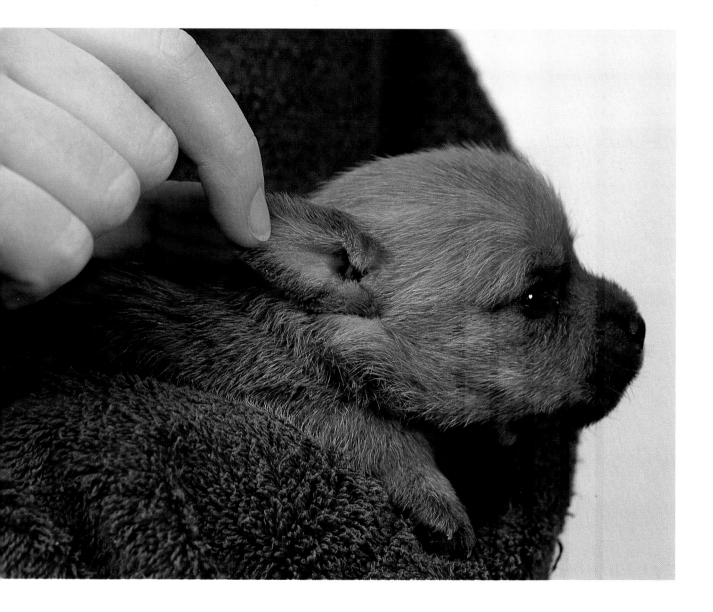

Every day Dolly grows.
She is two weeks old now.
Her eyes are open.
Her ears have opened, too.

She is a lot bigger,
but she still can't stand up
all the way.

I want to play
with my puppy,
but mostly
she wants to eat
and sleep.

She is busy growing,
so I leave her alone.

Now Dolly is four weeks old.
She is strong enough to sit and stand.

Then she takes her first step.

Soon she is running all over the place.

When Dolly was born, she had no teeth.
Now look in her mouth!
The puppies' new teeth hurt their mother.
She won't let them nurse as much.

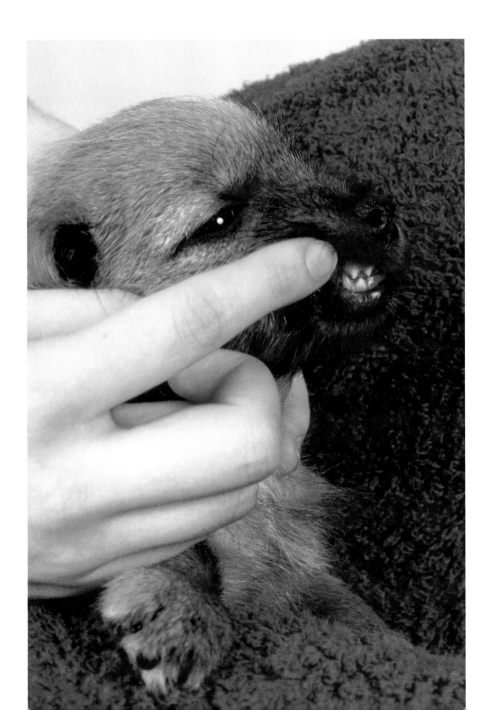

The puppies' first solid food is baby cereal.
At first, Dolly doesn't know how to eat.
She puts both feet in her dinner.

But after a while,
she learns to eat neatly.

Soon all the puppies are eating dog food.

Every day, the outside world
looks more interesting.

Now Dolly can get out of the box ...

all by herself!

The puppies learn to play.
They play with toys and other things.

They play with each other.

And they play with me!

After all that
playing,
it is time
to sleep...

and sleep...

and sleep!

When Dolly is eight weeks old, she is ready to leave her mother. At last, I can take her home.

I give her a dish . . .

a toy . . .

and a hug.

Now Dolly is
really mine, and
the fun is just
beginning.